TH

MW01596772

THE OVERGROWN COPSE

& OTHER POEMS

Jane D'Arista

Antrim House
Simsbury, Connecticut

Copyright © 2014 by Jane D'Arista

Except for short selections appearing in book reviews,
all reproduction rights are reserved. Requests
for permission to reprint should be
sent to the publisher.

Library of Congress Control Number: 2014902099

ISBN: 978-1-936482-61-0

Printed & bound by United Graphics, Inc.

Artwork by Robert D'Arista (www.robertdarista.com)

Image Design by Lowell Gilbertson

Book design by Rennie McQuilkin

"Message for Augustine" appeared in *Regrets Only: Con-
temporary Poets on the Theme of Regret*. "The Squatter" was
a finalist in the 10th Annual Inkwell Poetry Competition
and was published in the 2008 Spring issue of *Inkwell.*

Antrim House
860.217.0023
AntrimHouse@comcast.net
www.AntrimHouseBooks.com
21 Goodrich Road, Simsbury, CT 06070

For Bob

SPECIAL THANKS

During the years when work in another field absorbed most of my time, the encouragement I received from two friends and two family members was the critical support I needed to continue writing poetry. Most important were the almost monthly meetings with Elizabeth Stabler at a boatyard restaurant in Stonington, CT where we read and discussed our poems and enjoyed the pleasure of our shared interest in what we were writing and reading. Judith Herz was another frequent reader in those years as well as a friend willing to engage in long conversations about contemporary poetry as well as the poets she teaches and writes about. In addition, having two faithful readers in the family – my daughter, Carla, and my brother, Hank – was a very welcome affirmation of interest and support for which I was and am very grateful. And then there were the friends and neighbors who showed up for readings in the garden on summer afternoons. To them my thanks for their loyalty.

Several years ago, I joined the writing group at the First Congregational Church of Old Lyme and last year, thanks to Marilyn Nelson, became a member of the Connecticut River Poets. I am deeply indebted to all the dedicated poets in these groups for sharing their work and for the comments and responses needed to revise and shape this collection. Finally, I am very grateful to my editor and publisher, Rennie McQuilkin, for his interest in these poems and for making this book much better than it was when he received it.

TABLE OF CONTENTS

I. INTO THE BEGINNING OF MEMORY
("Flowers," Robert D'Arista)

II. THE LOTUS SEED
("Eggplants," Robert D'Arista)

III. SOLO
("Berkeley," Robert D'Arista)

IV. THE EUROPEAN ROOM OF MY MEMORY
("Interior, Rome," Robert D'Arista)

V. DEFACINGS
("Standing Figure from Rear," Robert D'Arista)

VI. WHATEVER IT IS WE CALL HOME

("Flowers II," Robert D'Arista)

Here I come the invisible man, perhaps in the employ
of some huge Memory that wants to live at this moment.

Tomas Tranströmer, "December Evening, '72"
(translated by Robert Bly)

A turn, a glide, a quarter turn and bow,
The stately dance advances; these are airs
Bone deep and numbing as I should know by now,
Diminishing the cast, like musical chairs.

Anthony Hecht,
"Saraband on Attaining the Age of Seventy-seven"

THE OVERGROWN COPSE

& OTHER POEMS

I. INTO THE BEGINNING
OF MEMORY

Finding a Field

She had never walked that road before.
It turned in an arc around a field
fenced with posts and loose strands of barbed wire –
for cows, she thought, no longer there –

just a faint dirt track through scrubby pine
near her great-aunt Ida's house in Callahan
where the families that farmed raised chickens,
kept a hog, a cow and a patch of corn.

The field's freshness seemed out of place –
tall grass of a different green
flecked with buttercups, daisies
and Queen Anne's lace. Small insects
rode up and down on a breeze.
Their flat song – a steady beat
where the flowers swayed – seemed to say:
This is the way a field should be.

She grew, moved away, never went back –
never knew if the field survived
the lava-like spread of the city.
The way it had been remained in her mind –
possessed even when forgotten –
part of what she saved and took with her.

The Name of What Was There

Autumn: Sumner, Georgia
for HTW

Flowers are killed by frost, they said;
falling leaves foretell the dying of the year.
But dying meant nothing to me until that fall
when we went back to the farm where my father was born
to see men kill what we took home to eat.

They had been working long before we came –
laughing, hoarse from shouting, voices drowned
by the roar of the fire. A boy no bigger than I
watched women heap plates with food and
pass them around. The men ate and returned
to the yard again and again – clubbing the heads of
squealing hogs in the pen, stringing them up
belly-bare against the barn. My father
put me on his shoulders, lifting me up
to see their throats slit.

                    I saw and heard
all I could understand – inhaled the odor
of sweat, burning wood and the sweetness of blood
with the cold night air. They seemed like clues to a riddle
as yet unsolved: the name of what was there.

At Watch Hill

A hotdog stand with wooden picnic tables
resting on uneven ground – the carousel
and rows of lockers guarding the entrance to the beach –
unfinished summer stretched all around
without a plan, without markers pointing
to where it began or would end.
Only the sun was keeping time –
and the music keeping pace with the painted horses
prancing up and down – and the heartbeat of a child
riding there, thinking only she
could feel that sudden surge of excitement, that fear.

The St. John's Jetty

The road to the jetty follows the river to its mouth
past marshes and streams where small boats
work their way through stands of grass.
The smell of water's treasures hangs in the air, rising
from wooden shacks that sell boiled shrimp,
smoked mackerel and raw oysters to shuck
and eat there.
                        Where the road turns
and heads up the Atlantic shore, the jetty
stretches out to sea – a wall of concrete
buttressed with stone that fishermen use to cast
into deep water; that tourists visit to see
sharks and dolphins swim on the ocean side.

In summer, sitting on a rock below the wall –
watching the naval base across the river
keep ready for the ongoing business of war –
I read my way through adolescent awakening
where the sound of waves enforces solitude.
Isolated, stark – frightening when water
swirls at my feet and I feel its pull – the jetty's
a place to step past what I know – a path
to distances, to worlds I want to reach.

The Way I Wanted to Meet You

for Carolina at six

I never wanted to meet you as one
whose presence you thought demanded a response.
I dreaded watching you bend to accommodate –

eyes alert, working to understand;
face focused on some question I framed
awkwardly, trying to get it right.

All I wanted was to stage the event –
make space for you to move and speak
so you could show the self you had become.

And I would come with fireworks in hand
to light that space around you – to project
a brilliant arc so you could see my love.

The Overgrown Copse

For Carolina

It is as if you have entered
the shade of an overgrown copse
at the edge of a sun-baked field —
the contrast seems so great from then to now.
Once there, the bird you hear singing
is the sound of your own voice, rising
to a note you had not known you had.
Your eyes move like fingers tracing the contours
of a face — fingers extend for the latching of hands.
Beauty is there to astonish: you see another
and feel you, too, are seen.
You did not know one could enter Eden
but know now it's where you are.

Whalebone Creek

for Thomas

Eels. We crossed the road to see them
spill into the pool at the base
of the waterfall, to watch them writhe,
massed together until pushed by the current
toward the brackish cove beyond.

I told your sister they would head
to the warm Sargasso Sea to spawn and die –
that an embedded memory would bring
their young back to these cold waters
and link the beginning with the end of their lives.

Of course, that was more than you
could understand. You were only three.
But, curious to see the eels,
you bent too far and fell
head-first into roiling water.

Your father shouted, lunged, grabbed
your ankle and pulled you out. How
that dark plunge felt you felt
again in dreams – a recurring baptism
into the beginning of memory.

Observation at the Beginning
of the School Year

What news of loneliness might that one tell!
So sure that someone will be watching,
he pulls up his backpack in an awkward ballet,
holding together whatever it is
that just might fall apart.

Not that he's one to complain. But,
should it escape, that long, low wail
inside could blow his life away.
Nor can he share; can't put himself
in another's shoes until he can fill his own.

But he is young and that will change
when – drawn by the sound of a voice,
the look on one particular face –
he reaches out for what he needs
to make his world a friendly place.

The Children

For Peter

Where they are in your life
you once were in ours.
Old photos show us standing,
hands on shoulders, the way
you stand behind them now –
caught in a place where lives
are redefined. You helped shape
what we became just as they,
small sculptors, will remold
your unfinished clay.
Soon – when growing up
becomes growing away –
they will take what you gave to take
your place – leave you changed
by what they made of you.

II. THE LOTUS SEED

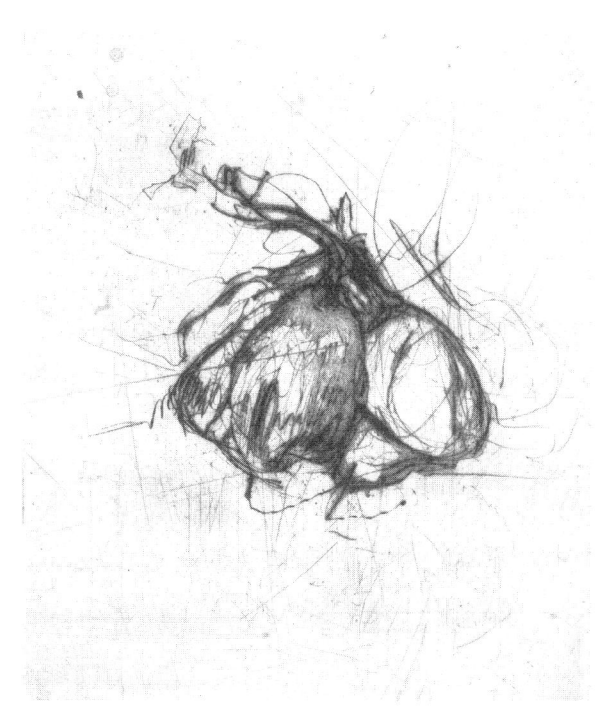

Out Walking

Do you remember when we walked the streets
looking for our would-be lover? Stopping for coffee,
buying a notebook, pencils, a box of paper clips –
seeming to have a purpose as in fact
we did: to see that face, be noticed, even
exchange a word or two – small pleasures
that failed to dampen desire. It remained,
driving us out to walk again – heading off
in this or that direction, hoping to find
where it was we were meant to go.

Girl with Long Hair

She had a weight of hair
and cared for it. Its bloom
was the all of her
for its weight dragged her down.

She could not rise above it.
She never rose and the rose
her hair made of her
faded into mist —
what the man in his journey
gently thrust aside.

A Brief Biographical Sketch

Clothed in the costume of his time
(confident he was merely playing
within the play), he cultivated
an intellect as well-contained
as a Swiss army knife – as versatile,
though useless beyond a certain range.

Accustomed to the assurance
of reward, he avoided tasteless pathos
or poverty. His was a life made to seem
enviable, serene – until, one day,
he lost his place in the script,
dropped some props and then a wife.

And then he knew he did not know
who he was or what to do or why.
It seemed best to do nothing
and continue to die.

The Squatter

Always, that old feeling squats outside
waiting to be let in. It knows about
the rain – knows that insistent sound
calls up the night you first saw
how easily I could be made to give
what you wanted – how quick I was
to shrink from anger, to placate.

For you it came to seem like play –
the threats not real so no real damage done.
But you coupled with the squatter in wait there –
the formless fear that others helped create
and I hoped you would chase away.

You Driving

The road slides beneath a bank of trees.
Sun and shadow flicker across your face.
You turn to smile and feeling surges
like the motor of the car we are riding in,
you driving. . .

                 Why does this one
of our many days together seem
so special now? What happened then —
that time when I felt so alive?

At Point Reyes

Looking across this dry basin
to the bay beyond, I try to imagine
what one would find below,
inside that cradle of power
we call the San Andreas Fault,
if one could go down to see it shrug,
groping for the right position before
lapsing into decades more of sleep.

After days living on this hillside,
the inner ground on which I thought
I stood begins to show fissures
of its own — cracked surfaces above,
unpredictable rumblings below —
signs of a shift that destroys as it moves
to renew, waiting out of sight
like the one here, hiding under the meadow.

The Lotus Seed

I was told this seed is very old —
it was found in a pharaoh's tomb, placed
to return with him in an afterlife
when it would bloom in a sacred pool
imagined by those who buried it there.

Lotus from other seeds in that tomb
grow in a water garden near
a bend in the Anacostia river.
I was told that mine would bloom
even if planted in my small pool.
But I put it away, planning to build
a larger pool — thinking that waiting
a year or more could not harm a seed
that had survived so many before.

I was, in fact, afraid to plant it —
afraid it might fail — that I would rob it
of its power to live into the future —
would lose the blossom planted in my mind.

III. SOLO

Seeing Muriel Again

*A photograph of Muriel Rukeyser appeared in the 1997
New York Public Library desk diary, "Celebrating Women Writers"*

I turned the page at the end of September
and you were there. Not just your photograph –
you, in a room I remember as white,
dressed to go out, saying what we should eat,
what read, and when I should turn out the light.

You were the age you are in this picture.
These are the same large hands, dimpled chin,
eyes cast down and to the side. For a moment
after all these years, I could hear your voice,
your laugh – even recover that part of myself
who thought she knew who you were
and did not.

       The next year
when your wedding present came –
a pair of crystal doorknobs – I felt the surprise
you intended, remembered your delight
in unique but simple things. In time, I saw
what I could not see before – your readiness
to commit, each day, to creating a life.

It stays with me now as I reach
the final frame of memory where
you take your purse, kiss your son, smile
and close the door – performing again
that trick you had of emptying a room.

Projection

I see a woman in a field somewhere,
in the only place she will ever know –
in a world so large her coming and going
leave fewer traces than melting snow.

She moves now and lifts her head. Hers
is not what is called a "plummet-measured face."
She limps, favoring some wound, and has a wall-eye.

Crossing the field to the river, she kneels to drink.
Her bent body suddenly seems flawless,
its beauty drawn from the life it holds.

If the wild poppies in this field
were stirred by a breeze, would what I see
and smell be the same if I were she?

I cannot know. There's a difference – a distance –
required for this tenderness I feel for her –
that I want felt for me.

The Curtain

Idle, listless on a summer day,
I watch the half-drawn curtain
hanging from a brass rod –
a shimmering foil for light that slips
ahead or behind the measured hour
to follow the capricious rule of air.

Unfurling translucent, rippling folds,
it assumes command – asks to be followed
as it billows away from the window sill.
The loosened pleats of fabric take wing
before collapsing like a tent
unmoored, like the expended spirit –
that woven thing that hangs within,
rising and falling again and again,
to test the stringent confines of its frame.

Remembering My Mother

My mother left her life remembering
a summer day. She felt the heat, the coins
in her hand – heard her father's voice and the bell
of the ice cream man. She remembered running, falling –
the stab of pain and the comfort that came.
Each day she called it up again:
"Papa," she asked, "can we go now?"

Eyes blind, face contorted,
fingers holding tight some piece of cloth,
she stood – when she still could stand – motionless,
held by memory – the light guiding her
into the silence through which she passed.

After Loss

The sun grew weak lighting a flat horizon.
An even-handed wind exposed all frailty.
Memory came often, charged like a magnet,
raking scattered thought into piles.

   The night they took him down the stairs
   I could not know and did not know.
   We cannot know what we do not want.

As time erased, reality thinned.
Days pooled their stagnant streams,
widening the deeper lake of night.

   Grace? It's not being moved to defy –
   living without knowing when you'll die.
   As a precaution, I'm shutting the door –
   no reason to ask why.

Solo

My love, what once we imputed
each to the other – the same
grace and mystery, embodied
in selves that possessed and were possessed,
that secret languages expressed –
we bonded in flesh.

       Pleasure with purpose,
that bond was made to last –
past the fragmented lives we made,
past death's parting of our whole in half.
I still am one of two. And you,
memorialized by your own hand,
are yet the object of my eye.

Sorrow's Pool

By day, the depth of sorrow's pool is hidden.
Sun and clouds flatten and color its face.
But in the dark, with color gone,
its measureless menace reappears.

This is a place where one can drown.
The opaque surface opens, takes you in;
numbness obscures the slide until, at last,
you know you may not rise again.

Having risen twice in a single life,
I know I would sink if claimed once more —
weighted now with all I've stuffed
in the sagging pockets of my heart.

Under the Quilt

I enter the tunnel under the quilt
and wait for the warmth to come –
one way to ease one kind of pain.
How long has it been since you left my bed
and I have lain alone?

Advice on Long-term Planning

Take all against a time of need.
It comes.
Assume there's no chance to rehearse or repeat.
There is none.
Love, but know the grip of love
can't hold —
"falling" is what comes after,
not before.

There is a line —
I can't remember when I crossed.
A future flew up in the air, burst,
and was lost.

Song for a Sleepless Night

Time passing –
     heart beating –
rhythmic as a solemn march.
     Don't listen.
Hear instead
     the wind, rising
without a plan,
     somersaulting
through trees –
     the unhurried noise
of all earth's freight
     borne in circular motion.
Enter that round,
     revolving O –
bend the line
     striving for destination –
make it the note of a song.

Needing Shelter

Whispers of rain
barely overheard.
A quiet wind fingering
tips of leaves.
Summer hesitates,
leaving but lingering,
Stalled in moist air.

Try not to think
it speaks of losses.
It does. All day,
needing shelter,
I thought: our life together
gave us that.

The Gift

Somehow, at the end of a mundane dream
about going here and there and doing
things not done, for no reason
suddenly, your face appeared.
You said nothing but the look in your eyes
sent a message that, waking, I still feel.

I know – I surely conjured this moment
to meet my need and needed how it came:
perfectly disguised as something given.
Even so, it could not have come
had I not seen that look before.

Burial Ground

The dates of death for one family
in this old burial ground fall
within the same short span of days.
Whatever the cause, all were taken together.
I wonder if any were left and, if they were,
how did they survive these losses?
Did they come back to stand
and grieve where I stand now?

I seldom go to places where
those I've lost are buried. Instead,
they are visited, one by one,
in memory. But today,
in this abandoned graveyard, my dead
came to me. There were so many –
crowding in all at once!
Each brought the grief I had felt
for each – a weight too great
not to crush the will to survive.

Then I remembered the night
my first child was born.
The Italian mid-wife used a word
we both could understand
to ask about the pain:
"Supportábile?" "Yes," I answered.
Most things are
if you put it that way.

Old Woman in the Morning

What calls her now that she is old –
draws her from dreams of stories already
told? Taut, as if strung between posts,
she waits to be sounded by the slide of a bow
vibrating to the measure of her will.

A slower beat, a minor key –
a frayed score marked andante –
an interlude, she knows, before
what she fears – some raucous note
struck randomly at the close.

IV. THE EUROPEAN ROOM
OF MY MEMORY

Arcadia at Ephesus

A broken marble road
    ends in un-mown fields.
Cypresses, randomly placed,
    guard acres of fallen stone,
disrupting the geometric plane
    of this once perfected space –
the market's measured floor,
    columns, arches and, beyond,
the theatre – erect, still drawing
    crowds to its topmost tier.

We who come –
    what have we come to find?
A dead city's beauty?
A haunting reminder
    that even cities die?

Here, death seems impersonal –
    present, pervasive, without sting.
It's continuity we celebrate.
Why, then, this shiver –
    here, in the heat of the sun?

Places where lives no longer are lived
    record no more than repetition,
erase all that once was personal.
Is this our deeper loss?
    Is it why we collect
our thoughts and deeds – store
    treasured arts, tell stories,

honor those we think
    the great of their time?
Can that assuage this barren promise —
    the future we encounter here?

North of Naples

for Tom

It is noon. August. Dry gullies shimmer
as if they were filled. Lizards scramble, pause
and disappear. A puff of wind from the sea
strays by, stirring the olives. Their color –
all color here – is bleached. Nothing
is vibrant but heat rising in waves from stone.

Once this valley filled with men. Bright flags,
glittering armor and weapons colored it.
Shouts and the clash of metal pierced the air.
Standing here after centuries have passed,
it's easy to imagine how the battle began –
the headlong rush, the meshing of bodies together.

But how did it begin to end? Who first
among the losers knew it was lost? Who,
if any, did pity slow down? When
and why did the living leave the field? How long
before what they abandoned disappeared, leaving
the sentinel olives to repossess the hills?

Today only the olives remain – and the heat,
forcing sweat from our bodies as it did
from theirs. Some small part of what they felt –
terrible thirst – is all we can feel.

Swimming Near Sorrento

for Angie and Carla

Out from a rock-strewn, half-moon bay
below a terraced cliff, breathing
the pungent smell of oleander,
weightless, immersed in the warm element
of rebirth, we circle and tread, resuming
an endless familial conversation
that treats as one the living and those
already gone – retelling stories
that smooth the ragged edge of time.

But time breaks the spell,
casts shadows that rob heat from the sun.
Tired, hungry, we swim back
to gather clothes spread on the beach –
silent now, eyes cast down,
drained by laughter spilled out of love.

The Fragile Peace of a Roman Night

High above the street of the four fountains
in our landlord's sheets, on his vacated bed,
we heard the crazy woman at two or three
split the muted noise of night with her cry
as if in a dream: *ASSASSINI!* Then silence.
Then the cry again.
                    Often her anguish
flowed out in a torrent of words – timed, savored,
rehearsed and repeated like lines in a play. Her voice
reverberated across adjacent roofs,
commanding attention, building to the piercing note
with which she ended – prompting us, too,
to seek release: a quick coupling to regain
our hold on the fragile peace of a Roman night.

The European Room of My Memory

The European room of my memory
opens on a row of trees with peeling bark
and yellow leaves that fall on cobblestones
across a square. Alone there,
I move on to crowded streets where
I once lived – where I am a stranger again,
trespassing in places others own,
passing people who belong to their lives
in ways I seem not to belong to mine.

Lights flicker on and conversations quicken.
Doors open and shut, releasing the odors
and familiar sounds of evening – beginning a ritual
in which I take no part – a language
once heard as music that now sounds shrill.

I come back to this memory to find
a place I need to reclaim – an abandoned cloister
behind blank walls of solitude.
Inside, estrangement empties out the space
that waits for my return.

Summer Solstice, London

Late light after rain all day.
Clouds break at the horizon,
the sun brakes its final slide –
lifting a colorless film from the city,
unrolling a sudden, lavish display.

I have wandered alone all day –
tired of wandering and being alone –
not wanting the company of others,
wanting my own – dulled by something
nameless – not pain, not even loss –
I taste the nausea of waste.

Stopping to rest, watching the river,
I almost miss the close of the day.
It comes as a moment so final – past
falling into present without pause –
and ends like a phase of life
one hoped would always remain.

The Emigrant

The water lapped rhythmically below,
between the ship and the pier. For a moment,
watching it, he thought he might not go.
"There is another boat next week," he said.
"I could wait – even decide to stay."

Saying goodbyes the night before,
he had anchored faces, rooms – the street,
the latch on the door – into memory.

A belonging that once gave pleasure
had grown stale. Anticipating the new,
the unknown, he would go.

Afterwards, he dreamed of the lapping water
and of falling – falling endlessly
between the moving boat and the pier.

Wonder

In Perugia that September, taking
refuge from the midday sun,
we stepped into a medieval world
in shadow beyond an open door.
There, gradually regaining sight,
we could see the ancient beams,
marvel at the way a vaulted ceiling
made the space above seem so large.

I felt the same astonished pleasure
as a child in another dark place —
an orange grove hugging the shores of a lake,
low-vaulted and dense with hanging fruit.
Emerging from its canopy
on a December night to stand
beneath the open sky, I was held fast
by the infinity of stars scattered
throughout the high, crowded dome
beneath which the earth is placed.

Moments when being moves beyond self
can never be conjured. Their magic
requires the trigger of surprise.
I saw such a moment again —
saw it come into your face —
when you waved me away as I tried to help
and gave yourself to what it took to go.

V. DEFACINGS

Meditation: King's College Chapel, Cambridge

Standing in an inverted nave
afloat in the arc of heaven,
where fanned columns extend the reach
of aspiration, soaring above
the choir screen Henry placed
to mark the ground with his passion for Anne —

I think of that lost lady
and many more before and after
who could not walk behind that gate —
confined by barriers of custom,
compliant to the purposes
for which their bodies were made.

Scorned, jealously held as possessions;
idealized, infantilized,
to increase and control their value;
reviled as breeders of death, disease and daughters;
begrudged their equal share in generation,
their voice in inheritance —

Even queens bowed in this
holy space, diminished by fear,
by the anger and disappointment of those
who blame injustice on divine
fate, accusing God to excuse
the worlds of pain they make.

And now, as then, the organ sounds,
ending our earthly meditations —

calling us to stand, to be present, to join
in a solemn act of communal remembrance
that celebrates the giving of the gift
for which this vaulted nave was made.

I step aside, ready to leave but hungry
for more — not for retribution or ending
injustices in which I, too, comply.
I want the promise of mercy — want it now:
an end to exile, Eden restored, for all
the right to know the worth of their creation.

Message for Augustine

I was surprised you were here,
near the house where you sent me to stay,
walking with those who follow you now.
Always before I was told you were coming
and could hide. Now that you are known,
I am known – and know myself –
as Augustine's abandoned concubine,
the fig they say you picked when ripe
and tossed aside to dry.

Believing you would think I sought you out,
I turned away – hiding from what you
could not help but show. Our life
is gone from your life – those days
we lived together so easily –
you – kissing my arm, tasting the salt
that excited you. Is that memory gone?
Will I never again see my face
cradled in the softness of your eye?

They say you are changed by love for God,
drained of self – dead to the life
I have had no wish to survive.
But isn't it selfish to think the past
is yours alone? To assume that I,
like our son, have passed from this world?
As you see, I remain – one who wants only
to hear you say the name I sign.
Say it.

Aurora

apologies to Pierre Corneille

Once, it is said, Aurora stayed so long
in Night's bed she kept the sun from rising.
Since it's her job to be his guide,
he hid – frantic – until she appeared.
Men made up stories to explain that strange
dark day. Some said the cold moon
stood in front of the sun to warm herself.
Others said the earth breathed fire and covered
the sky with clouds. None of that was true.
It was the fault of a lazy, wanton woman
who ignored her duty and indulged her ease.

Shostakovich at Oxford

The photograph shows a procession
walking in single file – wearing
ceremonial robes and hats
and led by a former prime minister –
going to be honored for what they have achieved.

The prime minister's stride is confident and proud.
The empire is gone but its trappings remain.
Framed by aging golden walls
with a swath of green behind his path,
he belongs, still belongs,
to the world in which he was born.

Outside this jeweled city, many
have long since lost the worlds in which
they were born. A gain for some –
liberation, perhaps – for others, a loss
too large to overcome.

Yet most of us can claim at least
a neighborhood – a place defined
by paths to follow – even though
it's only ours until we face
the choice to go or stay. Either way,
unlike the assured prime minister,
we may fall out of step
or lag behind – like Shostakovich,
caught at the end of that line.

The Beheading of the Baptist

Embarked on his final arc of flight,
Caravaggio painted this page
from the canon of their faith
for the Knights' oratorio in Valletta.

This is his last Baptist — no boy as before,
but young. His head, half-severed,
lies on the floor — his face lifeless
beneath strands of shining hair.
Those who gave the order for this death
are not here — only those who
must carry it out: the almost-naked
executioner (bending, grabbing the head,
a knife in hand behind his back);
a man with furrowed brow who points
to where the platter should be placed,
and the girl holding it, intent on her task,
extending the soft flesh of her arm
into the painter's signature shaft of light.

In the shadow, in back of that light,
an old woman struggles with horror and pity.
clasping her own head in her hands
while, on the side, prisoners watch
passively behind an iron grate.

After this Baptist, there was time to paint
more martyrdoms in Sicily
and here, on Malta, Saint Jerome writing
at an age the painter would not reach —

dazzling works that celebrate the body's beauty,
mourn life's too-short span
and stretch the reach of art to probe
the inner worlds these faces and gestures reveal.

The oratorio is a quiet place,
built to house timeless praise.
It holds this jewel of a timeless world
brief lives are used to make.

The Vienna Court Opera House

Photographed in the autumn of 1938,
the Vienna Court Opera House – its clock at noon,
its ornate facade unmarked by current events –
adds a receding period to the sweep of time
that measures earth-bound immortality.

Above its high porch, bronze horsemen rise against the sky.
The horses legs are lifted, and lifting their legs below,
pedestrians stride forward from opposing sides,
meshing as they cross at the turn of a light. A tram slides
between buildings whose signs say how they are occupied.

Intending, perhaps, to show a greater monument,
the camera fuses the complexity and order
that a city requires. But the lifted legs, the tram,
the clock up on its pole and the café sign
seem *mementi mori,* caught in a mocking eye.

The Vienna Court Opera House, at noon
in autumn of that year in black and white,
escaped with the photographer and survived
the bombing that defaced its facade
as an image in the Bettmann Archive files.

Ulysses S. Grant at the Capitol Reflecting Pool

Mounted on Cincinnati, Grant slumps
on a high pedestal at the foot of this hill.
His horse turns its head, lifts a hoof and
seems to move its tail as if to question
the immobile rider staring straight ahead.
Collar pulled up, hand on hip, hat
low on his brow, the General's shoulders sag
under what may be a drenching rain – or
the weight of accumulated victory, gained
by hoarding immense sums of collective loss.

On the ground below, a group of cavalry ride,
raising a trumpet to sound the charge.
Strained, excited, men press their limits
and the animals' speed. In front, a horse
and rider are falling – the first fatality,
coming before the battle begins.

On Grant's left, horses struggle to drag
a wagon and gun through deep mud.
Above stressed wheels, two soldiers
huddle against cold and the coming night.
Their faces show lives too long unsheltered –
homelessness that endures for those who survive.

Come. Walk here quietly at the noon hour.
Avoid crowds that come for inaugurations
or fireworks at Fourth of July celebrations.
Stand alone in this most public of spaces
to see the wound it commemorates
recast the field of triumph as defeat.

News of the Day

It's not easy to think of you –
all of you – none I know
but hear about as news – NEWS!
A few there, hundreds elsewhere
singled out for violent death
because of where you are.

So ordinary those places
that claim your forced slide
through the remains of what
binds the threads of life.
No boatman, no bell. You go alone –
leave a wraithlike image
adrift in a stranger's mind.

The Nuclear Power Plant
at Haddam Neck

For Thomas

Mist rises from the river.
A small dome protrudes through trees,
a secular temple – silent, abandoned –
guarding the soured prize of knowledge. Today,
the site of an accident. Small. Contained.

Down river, the hands of a woman clipping phlox
reach through scattered butterflies.
Crickets sound the bell of August,
calling in a summer overripe,
weighted with trophies of fertility.

A woman in a garden she has made,
nurturing life that ends in death
as will the life she received
and passes on. She, too, fulfills
a seasonal span in the covenant with time.

She fears that covenant could now
be broken – the forbidden fruit eaten,
the old expulsion become a prophecy.
She thinks it is only now
we can lose the garden we were given.

Armistice Day

For D.B.

Few who fought in that war are still alive.
Most of those alive now were not yet born.
But we, born between the wars, still remember
cold November mornings at eleven
when a siren rode the messenger air.
Arresting motion, commanding silence,
it signaled time to honor the rites of sorrow —

not only for them, those who died in the war,
but for ourselves: families on our block,
making do, losing inches at the edge
of better lives we had hoped would come.
Some fathers were lost to the ways shame
takes men without work, without pay —
mothers to the numbness of worry and strain.
Some grew up wild but there was no blame —
just sadness when things turned out that way.

Armistice Day allowed us to grieve —
to blend our pain into a hallowed loss.
The memory of that shrill sound
still speaks for us — and the silence
we kept to let it be heard.

VI. WHATEVER IT IS WE CALL HOME

Autumn on the Train to Boston

Stopped in a field of crimson:
sumac, edging along a marsh
where tall grass – feathered, burnished –
stretches leisurely out
toward the distant Sound.
There, the horizon draws an almost
visible line to seal water
from an enveloping sky.

The eye roams, defining its space,
finds the horizon – the last place
it can see, the place I
can never reach. Impatient now,
it scans the scene again and stops,
dazzled, in a field of crimson.

What's Left of Summer

For Sarah Enders Steffian

Outside, grey skies mute
the cornflower's blue. A last mowing
smooths the grass into light / dark rows.
Here and there a bit of gold
shines through: heliopsis,
rudbeckia, chrysanthemum —
what's left of summer, loosely held
on brittle stems and browning leaves.

Tomorrow may turn warm and fair,
reviving August's high-pitched light
to dazzle the surface of water,
deepen and distance the sky.
Still, the imprint of change will be there:
indelible marks etched on a plate
primed to show on darker days
when there is less — and it is harder — to see.

November

Yesterday's storm stripped the rest of the trees.
Naked and black, their limbs scratch a canopy
of restless clouds. Below, gusts ruffle
the heads of withered ferns, spreading a pallet
of fallen leaves. Burning Bush flashes
red and pink where barer shrubs bend
with the weight of birds. On the slope, deer graze,
stopping as we pass to gaze back.

It is now that the woods begin to stretch out,
their depth as measurable as a nearby field —
now that November slips in to close
the yearly cycle, springing its seasonal surprise,
prying open secrets summer had concealed.

The Porch in Winter

In winter the porch belongs to birds.
They hop on a bench that's mine in summer,
waiting their turn to pull seed from feeders
that hang on branches of lilac. A cardinal,

perched high on a limb, descends to join
a tenacious flock of chickadees;
jays and woodpeckers arrive, scattering
smaller birds across a glittering
ground of snow. Displaced by the bright
reds and blues of the larger birds,
the flash of muted color – black,
brown and striped wings; white
and citron bellies – recasts the scheme
of a vibrant, ever-changing tableau.

But these days are short, often grey –
usually spent doing what must be done.
At their end, when the birds return, their numbers
are fewer, their presence discreet as they
slip away to shelter – removed
from a world emptied by cold and night.

New England Spring

March freezes over once again,
arresting the advance of a ragged procession
formed in haste by a fitful tug of light.
When April beckons, the standard-bearers
cross into her terrain, reverse
brown banners and display new linings
stitched in muted tones of gold and green.

Days lengthen; buds swell; twiggy
lilacs turn to lace. Earth grows fragrant
pushing out life it sheltered from the cold. Warmth
parades like the tawny red of a finch's breast,
rising to his head like suppressed emotion.

Suddenly, without warning, a field trots
on to summer, defying the rule of the sun.
And the sun, inching to the top of his measured climb,
moves on – oblivious to the splendor he spawned.

Ashland in Moonlight

for Carla

The moon gains power as she moves into darkness.
Here, she sits outside the urban ring of light,
softening the night.
                    A house in shadow,
a garden at rest from its work with the sun,
my hands immobile, marbled against the rail –
shapes blur, change their size, altered by eyes
that strain to recognize.
                    Like the wise virgin,
the moon times her watch. She rises, slowly
passing the slower stars. The world below,
disarmed by her subtle command, lets go
the urge to define, the effort to explain –
succumbs to her knowledge of being to become
what will remain.
                    And I – like many
before me, many more yet to come –
slip into her orbit, fall in with her pace,
standing on a porch in the moonlight.

April Song

Days in April close slowly,
their descent into evening accompanied
by the falling note of a small bird:
"FEE-bee, FEE-bee" – the unique song
of the black-capped chickadee –
a voice of longing that calls for return,
points back to whatever it is
we call home.

NOTES

Titles of artwork in the book (all by Robert D'Arista, with image design by Lowell Gilbertson) are as follows: front cover, "Woman Walking," 1987 (collection of Jane D'Arista); back cover, "Figure in Interior," 1967 (collection of Klaus and Judy Preilipper); p. i, "Sleeping Figure," 1978 (The Watkins Collection, American University); p. iii, "Figure in Interior," 1973 (collection of Klaus and Judy Preilipper; p. v, "Self Portrait," 1984 (collection of Lowell Gilbertson); p. xi, "Sleeping Figure," 1978 (The Watkins Collection, American University); p. 3, "Flowers," 1981 (collection of Carla D'Arista); p. 13, "Eggplants," 1987 (collection of Klaus and Judy Preilipper); p. 21, "Berkeley," 1984 (collection of Carla D'Arista); p. 37, "Interior, Rome" (collection of Jane D'Arista); p. 47, "Standing Figure from Rear," 1983 (collection of Jack Boul); p. 61, "Flowers II," 1980 (collection of Stephanie Preilipper); p. 71, "Portrait of Jane," 1980 (The Watkins Collection, American University).

P. 29, "Under the Quilt." Two short lyrics by Robert Browning describe the arrival of a lover ("Meeting at Night") and his departure ("Parting at Morning") to meet his "need of a world of men." The voice in this poem is that of a woman whose bed, like that of the woman in Browning's poem, has been vacated. The poem uses mostly single-syllable words and the poetic devices characteristic of Anglo-Saxon poetry to describe her response to the shock of this immediate reminder of the loss of love.

In addition to her work as a poet, Jane D'Arista has served as an economist for the U.S. Congress and writes and lectures on domestic and international finance. She lives and gardens in Hadlyme, Connecticut.

This book has been set in Perpetua, designer Eric Gill's most celebrated
typeface. The clean, chiseled look of this font reflects
its creator's stonecutting work.

To order additional copies of this book
or other Antrim House titles, contact the publisher at

Antrim House
21 Goodrich Rd., Simsbury, CT 06070
860.217.0023, AntrimHouse@comcast.net
or the house website (www.AntrimHouseBooks.com).

•

On the house website
in addition to information on books
you will find sample poems, upcoming events,
and a "seminar room" featuring supplemental biography,
notes, images, poems, reviews, and
writing suggestions.